# Love That Lasts

## 7 Essential Habits
## To Maintain Love, Respect & Passion
## In Your Marriage For A Lifetime

### Grace Stevens

Red Lotus Books

# Claim Your Free Thank You Gift!

As a special "thank you" for buying my book you can get immediate access to my exclusive ebook

## Living Like Newly Weds

26 Amazing Activities to Maintain
Connection in
Long Term Relationships

Visit the One New Habit website at www.OneNewHabit.com and click the "Marriage gift" tab or type:

"http://OneNewHabit.com/marriage-gift"

# Table of Contents

# Why One New Habit?

Three years ago I started a book series called <u>One New Habit</u>. I have long been committed to personal development and being the best possible version of myself that I can be. I have spent over 20 years studying, reading, going to seminars and generally "doing the work" it takes to be a happier, more productive person and to have better relationships with myself and others. I am what you might call a "self-help" nerd. I've read the books, listened to the speakers, and done the exercises. A lot of them.

However, it occurred to me that very few people have the time or resources to follow the same path. When I examined the things that I had done over the years that had truly made a difference in my life it seemed that it all came down to the 80/20 rule - 80% of the results came from just 20% of the actions.

The <u>One New Habit Series</u> is about that 20% of actions. Rather than just give people mounds of information (fascinating though it may be), my goal was to give people a ROAD MAP. A set of easy to implement steps that, when turned into habits, would make a huge impact.

The books in this series are designed to be short, inexpensive, engaging and practical. They also contain multimedia components (if you read them in an ebook format) to suit different learning styles.

Let's face it, most of us have a stack of half-read books on our nightstand. My goal is to provide a book you can read on your phone or tablet during your lunch hour or listen to during your commute. Or even if you still prefer "old school," a book that would be dog eared on your night stand. A book you can and will finish reading. Tangible steps that you can follow. A book that you could easily revisit and find new ideas to implement that maybe you glossed over the first time. The goal being for you to adopt new habits. One habit at a time. The small 20% of actions that would make the huge 80% difference in your life. No weekend seminars or spiritual pilgrimages required.

Why specifically <u>Love That Lasts</u>?

The most popular book in the <u>One New Habit Series</u> is <u>One New Habit to Fix Your Marriage</u>. The book's goal was to give specific strategies to couples who were struggling to put the joy and intimacy back in their marriage. The overwhelming feedback that I received, however, was that the strategies in the book were good for *every* relationship, not just struggling ones. They were good relationship habits, period. But even more than that, I was impressed when people told me that parts of the book helped them with relationships with other people, not just partners - parents, teenage children, siblings, difficult co-workers and so on.

The message came to me loud and clear - people need help with relationship habits. Too many people view their relationship results as something passive, something that is just happening to them. For many people, learning that there are specific habits you could adopt that empower your role and results in relationships is new and powerful information. More, please!

Who Is This Book For?

This book is designed specifically for couples. All couples. Newly married couples, long term partners, same sex marriages, it doesn't matter. The relationship dynamics involved in growing together as a couple as opposed to growing apart are all the same. Even if you have been with your partner a while, you can (and should) pick these habits up at any time, not just at the beginning of a relationship. They are great habits that form the foundation for long-term growth, support, respect and on going passion in loving relationships. That's right. Adopting these habits can take you from honeymoon to "retired with grand kids" and beyond as a loving couple with the relationship everyone is jealous of.

Ideally, this book is aimed at setting your relationship up for success and helping you focus on your relationship BEFORE there are problems. Life happens, challenges come along, but if you have a solid foundation and good relationship habits, a marriage crisis needn't be one of them.

Honestly, my goal is to get this book into enough hands so that no one will need the <u>One New Habit To Fix Your Marriage</u> book :) Adopting these habits should ensure that your marriage stays healthy and vibrant, and will never need "fixing."

And it can be easier than you think!

Let's get started.

# Habit 1 - You Now Have A New Baby

Here's one of the nicest pieces of feedback I have ever received.

"Thank you for teaching me that love is a verb."

You remember verbs from school, right? Verbs are the "doing" or "action" words. Specifically, "love" is something you do, not something you feel.

This is an idea that many of you may be familiar with. The idea that actions speak louder than words. That you show someone you love them by what you do for them, not by what you profess to feel for them.

Of course, we all want to hear the words "I love you"." We all want to be told we're beautiful, appreciated and respected and expressing our feelings in such a way is important. But after a while words, if not backed up by actions, don't really set the stage for a love that grows. As pointed out by Tony Robbins, in the healthiest of relationships, we should embark on a mission "to give," not "to take."

*"Some of the biggest challenges in relationships come from the fact that most people enter a relationship in order to get something. They're trying to find someone who's going to make them feel good. In reality, the only way a relationship will last is if you see your relationship*

*as a place that you go to give, and not a place that you go to take."* Tony Robbins

So that's concept number one. Love is something you do. Hopefully that this is something you already know and experience in your relationship.

Here's concept number two. Your relationship is a living, breathing thing. It's a member of your family. Let me explain.

Are you aware of the expression, "the grass is always greener on the other side" ? So here's the plain truth about that. The grass is actually greener where you WATER IT. A relationship, like grass, needs nurturing to be able to thrive and grow. Without the proper attention, the relationship will wither away and die from neglect. Just like the grass. That's not a theory, that's a fact.

So the first habit you need to adopt is to think of your relationship with your partner as a family member. Someone who is living and breathing and needs tending to just as much as your children or even your dog. Because trust me, many people give their dog more thought and daily attention than the state of their relationship. Why? Do people not care about their relationship? Do they want it to die? Of course not! The reason people neglect their relationship is simple - they take it for granted, they think it will always be there. When life gets busy and there just aren't enough hours in the day to get to everything, the thing that gets neglected is their relationship. In their mind they already did the hard part, they found their life partner. Love should take care of the rest, right?

Wrong.

If you have read any of my other books you will be aware that this is a painfully familiar story for me. My passion to share good relationships habits was born out of personal pain. I watched a perfectly "good" 20 plus year marriage wither away from neglect. And that marriage was my own.

When people asked me why my marriage fell apart I had no good answer to give them. There was no abuse or addiction. No financial or health troubles. We had the big house, two great kids, two rewarding careers, and even the cutest husky in the neighborhood. Picture perfect. To this day, none of our family members have ever witnessed my ex husband and I arguing. Everyone was shocked by our divorce. And that included me, I'm embarrassed to say.

People like to delegate blame. Who was at fault? What did "he" do? Nothing. My ex husband and I were equally culpable of the biggest relationship killer out there - taking our relationship for granted and neglecting it.

Over the course of twenty years we had fallen into some really bad relationship habits. Separate bedtimes and bedrooms had started off innocently enough. I suffered from frequent insomnia and also get up at 5 AM to meditate. Sleeping in the guest room started off as trying to be considerate to my ex husband, and then ended up being the norm.

What I would describe as "tag team" parenting also just kind of developed over time. On the rare occasions that we all did stuff together (family vacations and holidays usually) we functioned very well as a family unit. But my ex and I had spent years without ever really cultivating sacred "couple time". My ex husband and I had lots of interests independent of each other and we got into the habit of "handing the kids off" to each other. "I'll look after the kids while you ride. You look after them while I go to yoga class." You know the drill. Communication between us was little more than texts delegating tasks and errands that needed to be run. Lack of physical intimacy just seemed like "a phase we're going through".

Now if you are a newly wed you are reading this and thinking, "what a idiot! How did she not see that divorce coming?" Bless your heart (and naivety) and I hope you never find yourself in the same situation. If you take the strategies in this book seriously and implement them then you are dramatically increasing the odds that you won't end up in the same situation.

But if you are ten or so years into a relationship and have gone through many of the "phases" when intimacy does lag, then where I found myself sounds a little more plausible. For example, after the birth of a child, when you have babies in the house, when there is a health problem or injury, when you feel depleted from looking after aging and dying parents. These are all times when your focus is more likely to be getting through the day in "survival mode" and intimacy just isn't on the priority list.

Of course, I suspected my marriage was in trouble. But I felt it was something we could "work on later", when the kids were older and out of the house and we had more time to give to each other. I thought my marriage was "a little sick", but could be saved at a more convenient time. But that was a complete misdiagnosis. The truth was that my marriage had flat lined. There was just no breathing any life back into the thing. There is only so long a plant can go without water. Drowning it in a bucketful of water after it's dead is not going to bring it back to life.

I hope I have adequately made my point here. Because I am not unique in this story. It's the story of many, many couples. And I don't want you to be one of them. Your relationship is a living entity. You need to prioritize it as such.

So is the title "You Now Have a New Baby" a little overkill? I don't think so. Not if you set the idea against the backdrop of our tabloid and reality TV culture.

For example, consider all of the pressure to find your "soul mate" and have the perfect wedding. TV shows like "The Bachelor" and "The Bachelorette" or even "Say Yes To The Dress" and "Bridezilla". Look at any tabloid magazine cover. As a culture we seem more focused on the actual wedding "event" than the relationship. Celebrity weddings (and, unfortunately their unravelling) are a national obsession.

With focusing solely on the wedding the subtle implication is that, once you've found your soul mate, you're done. I remember feeling that myself. Even though I chose a tiny courthouse wedding with no fanfare plainly stating "the marriage is more important to me than the wedding", I still had an overwhelming feeling of RELIEF. I remember feeling "I did it, I found my partner". I found the right guy. All that searching, all that wondering if it would "ever happen for me" was finally over. I'd done my job.

Even more damaging was everyone telling us that "the first year of marriage is the hardest". While certainly there were some adjustments to be made, of course the first year wasn't the hardest! My ex husband and I were crazy in love and still in the "honeymoon" phase! Try the year when you lose your job, the year when you're battling with postpartum depression or the year when doctor just found a possibly cancerous tumor in your 12 year-old daughter's jaw and the three surgeries that followed. Those were hard years.

But I remember thinking, again, after the first year "Hey, we sailed through that! Good for us, we're golden." No more effort required.

What would happen if we applied the same logic to child rearing?

Certainly the first year of being a parent is hard. I remember feeling totally relieved when THAT first year was over, too. I was so gloriously happy on my daughter's first birthday. After a year of constant second guessing myself and my parenting skills ( I remember crying "Why didn't this kid come with a manual?" many, many times) I had done it. My daughter was a beautiful, healthy, happy little girl. Although my wedding dress is long gone, I still have the dress and shoes that my daughter wore on her first birthday hanging in my closet. It was just such a wonderful celebration of family and friends cooing over my radiant daughter. It was truly one of the happiest days of my life. But it would NEVER have occurred to me that just because I had gotten through the first year I could cruise through the rest of my parenting career. We were just getting started, for goodness sakes! And I should have felt the same way about my marriage.

Your relationship will evolve, grow and change over time, just like your newborn. You need to tend to it just the same. Just because you found the right life partner, it doesn't mean you're "done". It means you are just getting started.

So that's habit number one. As goofy as it may sound - your marriage is like an additional family member. Hopefully the image of a brand new family member needing continued attention, love and guidance will stick in your mind. Your marriage is a living, breathing entity that needs to be tended to daily, not when you think you'll have more time (you won't find it) or more energy (you won't have it) or when "this phase is over" (it will be replaced by a new phase). This is the foundational piece of setting up a marriage for long term success.

## One New Habit - Sacred Rituals and Sacred Spaces

Develop a habit that helps you connect with your partner and strengthen your relationship every day. Here are some simple ideas:

1. End of the day ritual

Make it a habit to end every day with a short "sharing" ritual. Thank your partner for 3 things that they did that day that you noticed and appreciated. Once you "settle in" to a relationship grand gestures of love don't happen on a daily basis. But we still have a need to be appreciated and validated. A simple "I appreciate that even though you had a lot on your mind when you came home from work you took the time to help the kids with homework and load the dishwasher for me" may not be the stuff of romance novels, but it can go a long way in making your partner seem noticed and needed.

2. Honor a "Sacred Space"

Make sure there is a space in your home that is dedicated to just you and your partner. Usually that will be your bedroom, or at the very least, your bed. You should consider that space sacred, and a place that you visit together every day. Even if you work different shifts, make an effort to lay with your partner alone for at least a few minutes every day.

Also, neither technology nor children belong in your sacred space. I know this can be a subject that people get all worked up about. But if a child is sick or in need of you at bedtime or during the night, it's much better for your relationship if one of you goes into their bed and stays with the child there, instead of your children getting into the habit of sleeping with you in your sacred space.

With regards to technology in your sacred space. Many of us use our phones as an alarm clock. That's fine. Set the alarm, turn off sound notifications and set you phone face down on the bedside table. There is no good reason to be checking social media or e-mails while you are in bed, or playing Angry Birds or Words with Friends. Keeping technology out of your bed not only honors your partner and your sacred space, it leads to a better night's sleep. That's a proven fact.

# Habit 2 - Keep The Home Fires Burning

One of the greatest challenges in long term relationships is keeping the passion alive. And by passion, I mean engaging in physical intimacy on a regular basis where both partners feel sexually and emotionally satisfied. It is a tall order and requires work and commitment. But it is a very important component to the success of long term relationships.

Here are three commonly "accepted facts" about sex in marriage:

- It is inevitable that interest, frequency, and passion in love making will "die off" as a relationship matures. The longer you are married, the less frequently you will have sex.

- It is inevitable that sex in long term relationships becomes boring, routine and predictable.

- It is the male partner who complains that the burden to initiate sex always falls on them and that their partner is "never in the mood".

These myths are perpetuated by the media and late night comedians. Or maybe to you they seem like "facts" that have been proven by your own experience or the experience of other couples you know. But there is no reason for these to be the reality in YOUR relationship. Even if you have fallen into some bad habits, you CAN and SHOULD make keeping the passion alive in your marriage a priority. Why?

Here are just a few reasons:

Connection

Scientists will tell you that oxytocin (the trust and bonding hormone) is released during sex. I don't want to suggest that the "cosmic connection" you feel with your partner during and immediately after sex is just a chemical reaction. We are talking here about a connection with a person that you love. Someone you plan on spending the rest of your life with. Whether or not you believe physical intimacy is a sacred act of connection or not, it is an act that you share with this person and no one else. It is an act that should be unique to this relationship only. It is really important.

Stress release

Sex releases a whole bunch of endorphins and "happy" hormones that reduce stress.

Hormonal benefits

In addition to stress release, studies show that engaging in regular sex has additional health benefits similar to those of any other exercise such as increased longevity. In addition, sex can help regulate hormones resulting in a decreased risk of breast and prostate cancer as well as help reduce the symptoms of PMS.

Exercise benefits

Seriously, sex can burn calories and help tone your muscles. Female orgasms give a work out to all the muscles in the pelvic cavity which can help minimize the risk of incontinence as you age. Orgasms are certainly more fun than doing your Kegel exercises! And recent research also correlates regular male ejaculation to better urinary tract health and less need to urinate frequently during the night as men age.

Better sleep
Most couples know that there is no better way to fall asleep and stay asleep than collapsing relaxed and exhausted after a great sexual experience.

That "great sex" glow
You know that glow when you've had great sex? It's not just a myth. People who have regular sex are generally more relaxed, in a better mood and yes, their skin is better. Research shows that the hormone DHEA (Dehydroepiandrosterone) is released during sex. DHEA is known for repairing tissue and helping skin look young.

It's the best way to "affair proof" your marriage
I will talk more about affair proofing your marriage in a later chapter. But let me just say right now that one of the best ways to keep your spouse from straying is to make sure that your sex life is "healthy." And by "healthy" I mean exactly what I said at the beginning of the chapter - engaging in physical intimacy on a regular basis where both partners feel sexually and emotionally satisfied.

It just feels so good

You should enjoy having sex. Sexual climax releases dopamine, the "reward hormone." It stimulates that same part of the brain that gives you a "high" that can be synthetically produced by taking drugs such as heroine and cocaine. That's why people can become addicted to sex. But beyond the chemical response that sex produces in your own body, you should also enjoy the pleasure that being intimate gives your partner.

Good will

It just makes for an increased sense of "good will" all the way around. Often when one partner feels that they are not having enough sex, they tend to be more grumpy in general, and little resentments show up in all kinds of ways seemingly unrelated to sex. For example, let's say that something that bothers your spouse is the way you don't park straight in the garage or the way you load the dishwasher. Now, these are small things that are minor annoyances at best, not "deal breakers." But if you've been in a long term relationship you know full well that when the sex is good and frequent these "minor annoyances" slide by unnoticed a lot more than when the sex isn't happening. They have nothing to do with sex per se, but the tolerance level of these annoyances correlates directly to the overall satisfaction level of your relationship, which IS directly correlated to the quality and quantity of intimacy that you are enjoying as a couple.

Alright, enough convincing. Knowing that maintaining a healthy sex life is important is the easy part. The question is, how can this be accomplished with so many other priorities that you have to juggle every day?

Here are some suggestions.

1. Rethink the idea that intimacy equals intercourse

Understand that intimacy is a broad spectrum of activities and that the "end goal" of intimate actions does not necessarily need to be intercourse. I know that twenty years into my marriage I really longed for a time when a deep, passionate kiss could just be that - a deep passionate kiss and not an assumed invitation to have sex. Sometimes I just wanted a nice kiss and mini "make out" session with my husband without the pressure of going "all the way." If the kiss didn't lead to intercourse, I was left to deal with the "What did you lead me on for if you didn't want sex?" look and sulk. So eventually I just started to avoid the mini make out.

Again, intimacy can be a foot rub. A deep 30-second kiss. Spooning in bed naked. Intimate touching and stroking. And all of these actions can be intimacy WITHOUT the implication that it is foreplay. Intimacy of this nature has value and merit of it's own, whether or not it leads to intercourse.

Also, I don't mean to imply that it's just women who want little shots of intimacy and connection. I know more than a few men who complain that although their wives will have sex with them they very rarely kiss them and just "fool around" on the couch.

One of my favorite TED Talks is about this very topic. In it, Al Vernacchio claims that we need a "new metaphor for sex." He poses that discussing sex in terms of "going out to pizza" would encourage healthier discourse than discussing it in baseball terms.

Note - All the multi media resources I reference can be found on my website www.OneNewHabit.com under the "Book Resources" tab. Just click on the appropriate book and all the video and other links will be there.

So, back to the metaphor. Vernacchio explains that traditionally in America we discuss sex using a baseball metaphor. For example, we talk about "getting to first base", "getting to second base" etc. all the way through "scoring" or, if you don't have sex, "striking out." The baseball metaphor is not only used to describe heterosexual sex. For example, gay people are commonly referred to as "batting for the other team."

The problem with this metaphor, of course, is that it sets intimacy into the arena of competition. If there's a competition, there will be a winner. And as I explain later in this book, there can be no winner in a marriage. If one of you is winning, you are both losing.

Vernacchio makes a very compelling argument that a healthier way to discuss sex in a way that would invite exploration and promote satisfaction would be to use a pizza analogy. "What are you in the mood for tonight?" "What sounds good?" "How about half of this and half of that?" What if you don't necessarily want to go all the

23

way to intercourse (think of my kissing example)? What's wrong with promoting a little control and delayed gratification by suggesting, "How about we just eat half now and save some for tomorrow?" You get the idea. Now you're not having a competition; you're sharing an experience.

I know that some of you might think that it's just a metaphor. But language has power. And the problem occurs when the metaphor becomes the mindset. So whether or not you adopt the new metaphor, you should consider adopting the new mindset that says intimacy is a spectrum, and the "end goal" of intimacy should not necessarily always be intercourse. Sometimes we just want a taste, not the whole pizza.

2. The power of 20 minutes

One common problem that can lead to sexual dissatisfaction amongst women is not spending enough time on foreplay. From a purely biological standpoint, research shows that it takes a woman's body an average of 20 minutes of foreplay to be optimally ready for sex and orgasm. It's not simply a matter of being lubricated enough. During effective foreplay a woman's uterus moves up and back, the "erectile tissue" in the clitoris gets engorged, and the vaginal canal widens. All of these physical changes take time. The magic number is about 20 minutes. Remember, that's 20 minutes prior to penetration, not including the actual intercourse experience.

Here's the reality for many couples. They collapse into bed exhausted after their kids finally get to sleep and their responsibilities are done, and then the try to grab a few minutes of intimacy. It's easy to understand why many women in this scenario complain that the Intimacy they are experiencing isn't very satisfying. No one is putting the appropriate amount of time or energy into ensuring the woman is physically ready for penetration. Too often the focus of the "end of the day sex" is getting to a male orgasm as efficiently as possible. This means the man can go to sleep relaxed, and the woman can go to sleep guilt free. I know some of you will gasp at that notion. But the more uncomfortable that statement made you feel, the closer to the truth it probably is.

Trust me, most of us who have been married any length of time, especially with young children in the house, have been there. Being there once in a while is a reality. Getting into the habit of having this type (or lack) of mutually satisfying intimacy is very detrimental to the long term growth and vitality of your relationship. It is the breeding ground of resentment and dissatisfaction.

I understand that this notion of "putting in the appropriate amount of time" can be particularly hard for men to fully comprehend. In general, all a man needs to be optimally "ready" to have sex is any stimulus that results in an erection. This can be as simple as a touch, a stroke or even just the glimpse of nakedness. A man can be "ready for sex" in 20 seconds. That's not a criticism or judgment. That's a biological fact. And while this fact has served us well from the standpoint of ensuring the propagation of our species, it has not

25

served us well in the area of mutually enjoyable and rewarding intimacy in long term relationships.

## 3. How emptying the dishwasher is also foreplay

So far I talked about the physical side of intimacy. Women need 20 minutes of physical stimulation to be optimally ready for satisfying intimacy. What about mental stimulation? Here's where things get even more tricky. It's not so much that women need to have sex on their mind in order to relax and enjoy it, it's the fact that they need to have a mind free of other worries and concerns. Especially concerns in the area of care taking responsibilities. Seeing a pile of laundry unfolded on the bed, or the baby's toys on the floor can instantly kill an erotic charge in a woman. As best selling author and psychotherapist Esther Perel puts it, "Responsibility and desire just butt heads."

Pastor Ted Cunnigham explains this concept well by saying that "Men are like microwaves, women are like crockpots." He says that while men can be ready for sex in a second ("just show up naked"), women need support all day to get in the mood (just like food in a crockpot takes all day to be at its best). Not because they are not capable of being instantly turned on, but because for women "Energy equals sex drive."

In a speech to his congregation, Cunningham explains how he and his wife have a "crockpot candle" in their home. When he sees the candle lit in the morning, he knows that his wife intends to be intimate with him that evening. His job is now to support her all day so that she can be relaxed and relatively distraction and responsibility free when the evening rolls around. He helps her by getting the kids to bed, doing chores, making sure she has a little time to herself. He says that he loves seeing the candle lit because he gets to be an "all day lover" - sending her messages, making play lists, lovingly helping her with her responsibilities. He enjoys the anticipation, and so does she.

I'm not sure a crockpot candle would work for everyone. But the point is well made. Women who make it to the end of the day relaxed and having had a few minutes to pamper themselves are  much more likely to be open to intimacy than women who fall into bed exhausted and resentful that they get little support with household chores and have a pile of laundry staring at them from the end of the bed. Energy equals sex drive.

In my marriage, we didn't have a crockpot candle. However, many times my husband would encourage me to go out to the mall on a Sunday while he did the laundry and watched football. If I came home to a spotless house, laundry put away and kids fed…well, we both knew where the rest of the evening was pleasantly headed. We used to joke that the sexiest words he could ever whisper to me were "Honey, I scrubbed the bathtub." It's all part of the same idea.


3. Understanding the tension between stability and novelty

One of the biggest challenges to intimacy in long term relationships is the need to balance the appreciation of security, consistency, and comfort in our sexual relations without falling into the pattern of intimacy being overly predictable and routine. How do you keep things fresh and exciting in the bedroom and sustain desire over time with the same partner?

Belgian couples therapist Esther Perel posed that very question to couples in over 20 countries. The answers, along with 20 plus years of experience counseling couples, led to her best-selling book <u>Mating in Captivity: Unlocking Erotic Intelligence</u>. Perel concludes that the couples who succeed best at this have certain traits in common.

First, they make a rewarding sex life a priority.

Next, they understand that a certain element of unpredictability is crucial in sustaining desire. This can be accomplished in various ways through fantasy and role play.

Lastly, they understand that erotic desire, connection, and intimacy are all different things, each having their place in a successful union. Connection and intimacy come from closeness. But hot, burning desire can only come where there is a perceived "gap" to be bridged. To maintain this "gap" Perel advises that cultivating a certain amount of autonomy in a relationship is vital.

I will talk more about this final idea of autonomy in a later chapter. For now, let's get back to "Keeping things fresh."

Hopefully, you are not at a point in your relationship where lovemaking has become stale and routine. If it has, gently and playfully acknowledging the fact is a good place to start. You might be afraid that your partner will be defensive. In reality, they might be relieved you brought the subject up. You need to be diplomatic in your approach. Think back to the pizza analogy. You need to find a diplomatic way to introduce the idea of "Do you want the usual, or are you in the mood for something different?"

Something different? If fantasy and role play seem a little out of your comfort zone right now, you could start slower. Maybe try wearing or buying your partner new lingerie. See if that gets some conversations started. Or try gently experimenting with erotic toys. There was a time where such things were taboo and buying them involved an embarrassing trip to an adult store. Internet shopping has made things much more convenient. Even "mainstream" online retail outlets have many options for lubricants, toys, costumes, etc. Items of such a nature can be purchased, paid for and delivered discreetly and confidentially with no embarrassment.

Consider the phenomenon of the best-selling book Fifty Shades of Grey. Just a few years ago such a book would have been categorized as pornographic and fetish. Now it can be found at any major retailer, in plain view, being bought by soccer moms and grandmas alike. It has sparked a worldwide debate that is erasing the stigma surrounding fantasy and role play.

Again, every couple will have a different comfort zone. In the free Living Like Newly Weds guide that came with this e-book I listed some "sexy" date ideas. One of my favorites is recreating erotic scenes from movies. You could blindfold your lover and feed them food, like in 9 1/2 Weeks. Or come up behind them while they are washing dishes and make it an erotic experience before whispering in their ear that you are going to take them right there by the sink, like in Fatal Attraction. Watching the movie first together can go a long way to igniting a little desire. Then the surprise and anticipation as you start reenacting the scene should certainly chase away any notion of "Here we go again."

So you get the basic idea. Predicability and routine in the bedroom are safe and comforting and grounding. But for a healthy sustained desire, you need to mix in an element of novelty and surprise in your love making. Maybe for you, that's making love with the lights on. Maybe more. But making an effort to break out of your "regular" intimacy rut is key.

4. Avoid the "downward spiral" - go ahead and eat with your partner, anyway

Let's go back to the pizza analogy. Have you ever had the experience where your partner said, "Let's get something to eat" and you weren't hungry? You probably agreed to go eat with them to keep them company. But then maybe when the food came, and your partner started to eat, it just looked and smelled so good that suddenly you wanted to have some? Well, it can be the same with intimacy.

In my book about fixing struggling relationships, I made the point that putting intimacy back on the menu was really important. I used the eating analogy then, quoting the Italian proverb "l'apetito vien mangiando" (literally, "Your appetite comes when eating"). I knew from my own experience and the advice from many relationship experts that this was true. Recently I discovered a scientific study and evidence to back this theory up. The study was conducted by Dr. Rosemary Basson, Clinical Professor in the Department of Psychiatry and the Director of the University of British Columbia Sexual Medicine Program. Here's what she and her colleagues found.

Basically, the human sexual response cycle goes through 4 specific stages that can be categorized as:

1. Desire
2. Arousal
3. Orgasm
4. Return to normal resting state

Dr. Basson's research showed that for millions of people steps one and two are often reversed. The arousal leads to desire. Her research showed that, in general, men's response is more linear - going from step 1-4 in a straight forward fashion. However, for many women the progression through the stages was much more circular, citing "multiple reasons for initiating or agreeing to sex." Women may have initiated or been open to their partner's advances more for a desire for connection, or closeness, but then found themselves in the "desire" stage once they became physically aroused. The appetite came once they were eating, even if they weren't necessarily hungry to begin with.

Please understand that my goal in this book is to help you keep the amazing love that you already have with your partner alive and fresh. If your relationship is in a less than perfect place, then please understand that I am not advocating conceding to your partners desires out of a sense of duty, guilt or just to keep them from sulking. If your partner has been neither pleasant or supportive in general, or if they have been uninterested in your welfare or company all day, then just "saying yes" to their advances and hoping you'll "get in the mood" probably won't be productive. Other issues are festering and need to be addressed (outside of the bedroom). What I'm suggesting here is that if things between you are going well, and you want to keep it that way, try to remain open to your partner's advances even if you do feel exhausted, a little bloated or achy and would just rather go to sleep already. Because not remaining open could result not only in you missing out on some awesome sex, but is the breeding ground of resentment. Let me explain.

No matter how much confidence in themselves and your relationship your partner has, making intimate advances to you opens them up to a certain level of vulnerability. If their advances are not well received, it can lead to feelings of hurt and rejection, even if that was not your intention. Once someone feels hurt and rejected, they are less likely to feel loving towards you. Resentments grow. Not everyone has the emotional maturity or self-awareness to understand their feelings. Pretty soon, if advances are repeatedly turned down, you can find yourself in a downward spiral of rejection, resentment and negative thinking such as "Why does it always have to be on your terms?" or "Why would I want you to touch me if I'm angry at you?" This is neither a happy or healthy place for a relationship to be. Pretty soon your partner could stop making advances altogether. Lovemaking will get less and less frequent. And NOT having sex will become a habit. And not the type of habit that will set your relationship up for long term success.

## One New Habit - Sacred Acts

1. This one is straight to the point. Put pizza back on the menu tonight.

2. If you have time, watch Dr. Ester Perel's TED Talk

Or Ted Cunningham's talk. Again, the easiest way to watch them is to go to www.OneNewHabit.com and find this book under the "Book Resources" tab. All the links will be right here in one place.

# Habit 3 - Keep Dating Each Other

A recurring theme in my writing about healthy relationships is the theme of "connection." I have said many times that what is lacking in great relationships is not usually communication (my guess is you know how to complain to each other and delegate tasks just fine) but CONNECTION. When my marriage started to deteriorate after 20 years, I can honesty say that it wasn't that my ex-husband didn't understand what I was saying and thinking (lack of communication) it's that he just didn't care. That's because the connection between us was gone.

What do I mean by connection? Connection is that special bond and that chemistry that connects you to your mate in a way that is unique to a romantic relationship. The way that you are connected to the person you love is different from the way in which you are connected to anyone else. Part of this comes from attraction, shared intimacies and shared experiences. Part of this comes from having made a sacred commitment to your partner that you will share your life with them and create a partnership together where you will both value each other and continue to grow. And part of this comes from the many things you do on a daily basis to recommit to and nurture that commitment ("watering your garden").

So let me give you an example. When you text your partner and remind them to pick up the dry cleaning on the way home you are communicating. When you text them something fun or flirty, a favorite picture of the two of you or a reminder of an inside joke that you share just to make them smile, then you are connecting.

Research has shown that one of the best ways to keep "connection" alive in a relationship is through activities.

Note ** If you downloaded the Living Like Newlyweds ebook that was a gift with this book then you essentially already have the rest of this chapter. This chapter is a condensed version of that book laying out ten great activities. The Living Like Newlyweds ebook contains over 25 activities in it, and I highly recommend that you download it at your convenience. It will give you enough creative activity date ideas for over a year if you do one every two weeks. Because not every activity will appeal to you, the more ideas you have the better. Again, the ebook is FREE, and you can get it by visiting www.OneNewHabit.com/marriage-gift/ ***

OK, back to what I was saying. One of the best ways to keep connection alive in a relationship is through engaging in activities together. Not talking. Because most communication and "talking" likely involves talking about shared responsibilities, the delegation of tasks, details of your home, your finances or your children. Talking is important, don't get me wrong. But talking in long term relationships usually is for the sake of communication, not connection.

Remember when you were first dating? One of the characteristics of the early part of a relationship for many of you is probably that you would talk with your loved one for hours. You were so excited to learn all about them, their history, their passions, their dreams. But by the time you are a couple of years into a relationship, those conversations rarely happen naturally. At most, you will talk together about shared interests in sporting events or books or movies that you have enjoyed. But the "mystery" element in learning about the person you love has usually gone. And those conversations that you used to have, where you were learning about each other, were how you connected through talk.

So that's reason number one - the "connection" conversations have gone.

And reason number two is also very important. That's because "connecting by talking" is a very female way to connect. Men connect more by "doing", engaging in an activity together than by talking. If you have been in any longer term relationships, you will have figured this out by now.

In his best selling ebook <u>Catch Him and Keep Him</u>, Christian Carter explains,

*"Men love to be active and to play. They were raised to express themselves and connect with those around them through action. Unfortunately, too many women seem to forget this and want to talk their way into a man's heart. But the fact is that men don't "feel it" for you because of what you say. It's not your words that make a man attracted to you; it's the experiences you create with him."*

Why the "Date Night" Rut Doesn't Work

This is why the dreaded "date night routine" DOES NOT WORK. As any couple who has ever sought the advice of a counselor or relationship professional knows, spending "alone time" with your spouse without your kids, or other adults or members of your family is really important. It's a priority that you need to "schedule", otherwise it will get lost in the shuffle and business of everyday life. Therefore, many smart couples schedule a weekly or bi-weekly "date night" where they go out to dinner or a movie alone.

But if you are not careful, sooner or later date night becomes a chore. Because it is scheduled and predictable (i.e. 99% of the time it will be dinner or a movie), it just becomes one more thing you need to do. The responsibility for deciding what to do most likely falls on the same person every week. (Surprise! It's the one who stays home most of the time with kids and can't wait to get out of the house). Pretty soon it becomes a weekly "catch up on stuff" date. When there are young children present in the home, it can be hard to grab quiet time to talk. What inevitably happens is that "conversations" get put off until "date night". And they are not typically the "What are your hopes and dreams and how can I help you achieve them?" type of conversations, but conversations that are a recap of the frustrations, challenges, and drudgery of the week.

So, let me repeat. Talking is about communication. What will keep your relationship alive, vibrant, exciting and growing is not communication, but CONNECTION.

And connection comes through engaging in new and fun activities together.

The Even Better News About These Activities

So by now you should be convinced that engaging in meaningful activities is important. But how? Who has the time? Who has the money? Many couples face one or more of the following challenges: young children in the home, partners working different shifts or discretionary income for items such as date nights being very limited.

Good news! All of these sample activities I am going to list below are designed to be:

- low cost

- easy to do

- good, clean fun

- low commitment - meaning you don't need to buy anything "special" to do them. In fact, I designed many of them with the idea that you could **do them at home** after the kids go to bed.

Can't afford a baby sitter? No problem.

Many of these you can do at home. One solution could be to set up a baby sitting "swap" with a friend or neighbor who has kids around the same age. Not only will you get a night off every once in a while, your kids will LOVE it! Everyone wins.

OK - so enough convincing you *why* you need to make fun, activities part of your relationship. Probably you know it's a good idea, but you lack creative ideas.

Below I list several examples. Commit to trying one right away. Share the list with your partner and let them pick one. Set a firm date for when you will try the first activity. I think it is important to set up a schedule or at least commit to how often you will try an activity. There are plenty of ideas here, so there is no danger of falling into a "date night rut".

Here are 10 sample activities to get you started.

1. Go to the "drive ins"

Depending on your age, you may or may not remember that a trip to the "drive in movies" was long considered the ultimate "make out" date. But most drive ins movie theaters are either gone or really run down. They hardly scream "romance". But why not recreate the experience at home? It will be more romantic, more convenient and cheaper. The added bonus is that if you have young kids, you can have a whole "family date night". Do a double feature. Have the kids join you for the first movie, and then after they have settled down in bed, put on a romantic or "racier" movie and relive the innocence of a good old fashioned "make out" session.

To recreate the "drive -in" experience at home simply pull your car or mini van into the driveway. Put down the seats as needed. Set up a laptop or iPad/tablet in the vehicle. Add speakers If needed. Be sure to have popcorn, movie candy and sodas. If you are including the kids for a movie, you can all wear your pajamas for extra fun.

2. Spa night

Arrange a romantic spa night at home. Run a bath for your partner. Be sure to use bubbles and set the mood with romantic music and candles. Put towels in the dryer just before you use them to make sure they are warm and inviting. If you are a guy, maybe have a romantic new robe or nightie laid out on the bed for your love. If you're a girl, be wearing something alluring and romantic. Really focus on making your partner feel pampered. Lather their body. Wash their hair.

Extra credit. Finish off the evening with massages for each other.

3. Recreate your first/memorable date

Invite your partner out for a date. Be vague. To the best of your ability, recreate the circumstances of your first or most memorable dates. If it was pretty recent, you could even wear the same clothes. Make a playlist of "your" songs from your early dating era for the car ride. You can have fun seeing how long it takes for your partner to catch on.

4. Antique gift hunt

Go with your partner to an antique store or used book store. Challenge each other to find a unique gift within a modest budget ($10 or $20 should be plenty). Maybe split up and plan on meeting at a coffee shop or wine bar an hour later with your gifts. Be romantic...splurge for the gift wrapping service!

5. "Black out" date

This is a "stay home" date where you pretend that the power is out. No lights, no electronics or cell phones. Find your way around by candle light and amuse each other just by talking and touching with no other distractions.

6. The water date

Get out and about and take your date onto a body of water. There is something magical about water. You don't need to be on an exotic beach to find romance or on a gondola ride. Any body of water you can get to will do! Rent a pedal boat, a kayak or a canoe. Make your way to a deserted shore. If you can rent a pontoon, pack a picnic.

7. Take a dance lesson together

Find a local dance class. If "Dancing With The Stars" inspires you, take a ballroom class. If not, try a salsa or tango class. You could even try line dancing, if that's more your style. Anything that has you learning and laughing together.

8. "Make a wish" date

Make a list of all of the fountains in your community. Don't know where they are? Do some research beforehand. You usually find them in parks, by public buildings or in downtown retail areas. Now grab your loose change.

Make a fun afternoon or early evening date to visit every fountain with your love and make a wish at every stop (that's what the coins are for). You will increase your fun by giving extra change to children or strangers and encouraging them to make a wish, too.

9. Gourmet dinner night

Take turns with your partner setting up a romantic dinner date at home. If you set it up for every other week and alternate turns, that's only once a month that you need to be in charge. Dress up as if you were going out to a fancy restaurant, set out the best table linens, candles and turn on romantic music. Some advantages of doing romantic dinners at home are:

• much cheaper than going out to eat

• both of you can drink without worrying who will drive

• no babysitter, no problem. Have a light snack with your kids for dinner and have your meal after they go to bed. Seriously, one of the best meals I ever had was at 11.30 PM at night because my love couldn't start preparing it until 9 PM when the kids were finally down

- you don't even need to worry about getting to the grocery store. Most grocery stores deliver your groceries with a day's notice.
  Don't know what to prepare? The internet has thousands of gourmet meal ideas for every skill level, eating program and budget along with step by step YouTube videos on how to prepare them.

There. That was an answer for every excuse you had, right?


## 10. Build a fort

Embrace your playful side along with your passion for nesting together. Not everyone loves to camp (please, sleeping in the dirt is NOT for me), but everyone loves to build a fort. Use blankets, cushions off the couch, sheets, furniture. Whatever you need. Once it's built, sneak in together with a flash light and read to each other. Read romantic poems or, if you prefer, how about a little erotica? Either way it could easily evolve into a good old fashioned "make out" session.

If you have kids in the house, wait until they have gone to bed to build the fort. Leave the fort for them to find in the morning! Guaranteed they will be thrilled. Let them crawl in there with their breakfast and enjoy it all morning. That way you can have a fun "family activity", and you can enlist their help with getting the fort dismantled and your house put back together.

## 11. Scavenger hunt date

Men in particular love the thrill of the chase. It's biologically hard wired into their make up and, whether they were aware of it or not, was probably one of the things they loved about your courtship. Help recreate that thrill with a "scavenger hunt" date. Leave clues for your partner to follow that tells them what kind of attire they should wear, where to meet you and at what time.

## 12. Recreate a romantic scene from a movie

Here are a few examples to get you started.

For the pinnacle of romance, recreate the scene from The English Patient where Julia Ormond leaves a trail of tea light candles for her lover to follow (if you haven't seen the movie, put it on your date night movie list! It's a romantic staple).

For something sweet, how about recreating the spaghetti eating scene from Lady and the Tramp?

If you want something less innocent and more erotic, how about the blindfolded food eating scene from 9 1/2 Weeks? Whatever your mood, there are plenty of scenes out there to have fun recreating.

One fun idea might be to watch the movie as a "drive in" date one night and unexpectedly recreate the appropriate scene from it "unexpectedly" on a later date. That way your partner knows what's going on and doesn't automatically think you've lost a few marbles :) Also, think "small and intimate" here. No one expects you to be recreating scenes from Titanic.

Ok, so hopefully you are getting the idea of what an activity date that reinforces connection looks like. It is critically important to keep "dating" your partner in this fashion. Most couples think this "dating" stage of their relationship is over when their official courtship ends, but it shouldn't be. Continuing to create shared experiences together as just a couple (not always as a family) is an essential part of keeping love alive and nurturing your relationship.

And remember, if you enjoyed these examples, be sure to download the Living Like NewlyWeds guide for many more creative, fun activity date ideas.

## One New Habit - Sacred Time

Pull out the calendar. Start scheduling in activity date nights. These are "sacred times" that do not get rescheduled unless there is a real emergency. Avoid the temptation to think you "don't have time" for these dates. Let's be clear. What you really don't have time for is a marriage crisis and marriage counseling, and that's what will happen to your marriage if you neglect this type of "nurturing".

45

# Habit 4 - Teamwork Equals Team Talk

This habit may seem like an obvious one. You and your partner should be considered a cohesive "unit". You should present a united front to family members, friends, and in public. You should live with the confidence that your partner always "has your back". Sounds simple, right?

The degree to how obvious this advice seems to you will depend on how far into your relationship you and your partner are. Newlyweds are saying, "Of course, we know this, that's why we got married." Couples a little further into their life together might recognize the reality that family gatherings, evenings out with other couple friends, and even trips to the mall, can contain multiple opportunities for you to undermine each other if you are not careful.

So, remembering that this book is about practical habits and not just general advice, let's examine some solid relationship habits as they pertain to "Having your partner's back".

Presenting a united front in public:

If you disagree on something, agree to wait until you get home to discuss it at length. Whether it's the color of a new sofa or your opinion about your brother's new girlfriend, it is important to back each other up in public. It's far better to defer from giving a firm opinion by saying, "we're going to have to discuss this together and get back to you" than to argue in public. Not only is it damaging for your relationship to disagree in public but, as a general rule, I'd say no one enjoys being around a bickering couple. It's just awkward for everyone.

Making social and other commitments:

In many relationships, the woman naturally falls into the role of "keeper of the social calendar". In my marriage it was a joke that if my ex-husband's family wanted to schedule an event they called me to get it on the calendar, not him. Even if the role does naturally fall more with one partner, don't fall into the bad habit of agreeing to joint commitments without checking with your partner. There's nothing wrong with saying, "That sounds good but let me check Jim's/Jane's plans and get back to you." It's a way of being respectful of your partner's time and opinions.

Now, of course, if your partner is unable or unexcited about the social commitment then it's important that you don't "throw them under the bus" by divulging this. A simple, "I'm so sorry but I checked with Jim/Jane and it turns out WE won't be available to do that" will do. Remember, you're a team. Present a united front. If it's something that you really want to do and your partner doesn't and they are fine with you doing it without them, just be gracious. You can say,

"It turns out Jim/Jane is not available but I am, and I would love to join you. Is it OK if I come alone?"

There is no need to divulge that your partner doesn't want to participate. Smart and gracious people will not inquire further as to why your partner is unavailable and, if they do, a vague "they had a previous commitment" should suffice.

Your partner is now your "family":

When you got married, you and your partner created a new family unit. This is true even if you do not have children. It is important to remember this when discussions or tensions come up with regards to "my family" and "your family". If tensions arise and lines are drawn in the sand, you should not be standing with your family on one side of the line and your partner standing on the other side with his or hers. You should both be standing off to the side, as a separate family unit.

No airing of "dirty laundry" in public:

This should be a given. Problems or disagreements that you may be having should be discussed in private. It's a truly destructive habit to wait until you are surrounded by family and friends to bring these issues up, hoping that people will take your side over your partner's side. You might justify this behavior by saying that you just want "other opinions". The truth is you will only be receptive to opinions that back up your own. You will only succeed in making your partner feel betrayed as well as making those around you feel uncomfortable. If you truly need counsel on a problem in your marriage seek professional advice, or call a friend or family member to discuss it in private.

No passive aggressive criticism disguised as "teasing":

There is also a fine line when teasing your partner in public. Being playful is one thing; waiting until you have other people around to criticize your partner is another. No one is fooled by the claim, "I'm just teasing! You should be able to take a joke!" When you criticize your woman's weight gain or fashion sense or your guy's inability to fix things or earn a great income, it's not teasing. It's criticizing them in a passive aggressive way.

Again, the end result is your partner feeling betrayed and embarrassed and those around you feeling awkward. You should be aware that words have power. Even if you just think you are being funny by referring to your partner as "the old ball and chain" or "the boss", it's a bad habit to get into. Language such as this is disrespectful and subtlety damaging to your relationship. Leave that kind of talk to the comedians and late night talk show hosts.

When "venting" becomes bad mouthing:

Women, in particular, understand that sharing our thoughts and feelings is important. It fills a deep need within us to be heard and understood. A lot of times we process what is going on in our lives by talking about it.

Now, if you have been in any relationship for a while (or even observed your parents communicating), you will understand that there can be a problem with this. Often when we get home from work, women want to share details about our day, and get understanding. A little
49

empathy from the person you have chosen to share your life with doesn't seem so much to ask. Men, on the other hand, aren't all that keen to either talk about their day, or to listen about ours. Their primary goal in communication is not to share but to problem solve, fix the situation or give unsolicited advice ("Why didn't you just do or say XYZ?"). Basically, they just want to get the conversation over with as soon as possible.

I know from experience how frustrating this can be. In fact, I still get irritated at the memory of all the times my "sharing" about my day was interrupted with the words, "Can we please just have the short version of the story?" or the very masculine, "If you didn't want my advice why did you bother telling me?"

This is not to say that men are wrong and women are right. It's just to say that men and women communicate very differently. There are many reasons for this. Some reasons are based in evolution; some are based in body chemistry, different brain structures and the release of hormones. The topic is too long to fully explain here. If you would like specific information on this topic, I highly recommend any of the best selling books by Dr. John Gray of the <u>Men Are From Mars, Women Are From Venus</u> fame. Dr. Gray's work is very comprehensive and includes over 17 books. For a fascinating overview of his findings you can watch his 2012 TED Talk. His two "takeaways" for communicating with your partner at the end of the talk alone could make a world of difference in your relationship with your partner. Dr. Gray is just the best possible resource and I highly, highly recommend all of his work.

OK, so back to the point I was making. Because many of us have experienced this communication disconnect for ourselves, we fall into the habit of saving our "venting" sessions for when we hang out with our hairdressers, girlfriends, or guy buddies over a beer. Actually, not too many guys have venting sessions over a beer. They are more likely to be discussing sports and such. So if I'm totally honest, this little section is more for the ladies. But the fact is, we talk about our partners with others. And while this habit does fulfill an important need, it can turn toxic when it turns into chronic complaining about our partner.

The habit may start off innocently enough. You may be looking for understanding, empathy, and validation ("Can you believe he said that?"). But if it turns into constant criticism and complaining about your partner then it can be very damaging to your relationship. If you are truly seeking someone's advice on a particular situation, that's different. But if you are just complaining and "venting" about the things that your partner does that drive you crazy then you are violating your vows ("to honor and cherish") and being disloyal. Worse, you are focusing on what you don't want in your relationship, not what you do want. That creates a bad "vibe" that stays with you long after the venting session is over. It's a negative feeling that subtly permeates into your interactions with your partner when you get home.

Chronically complaining about your partner to others is quite simply a toxic habit.

## One New Habit - Sacred Words

1. Be mindful of your language. Ask yourself honestly, "am I teasing or criticizing?"
Eliminate "absolutes" ("never", "always") from your vocabulary, especially when arguing.
There will be more on this in a later chapter. Learning to go from conflict to cuddling, otherwise known as "fighting fair", is a really important habit for relationship success.

2. Make the commitment to present a united front in public and to "have your partner's back", focusing on all of the areas outlined above.

3. Examine your habits regarding "venting". If a trip to the hair salon or a guys' bowling night have turned into routine areas where you constantly vent about your frustrations with your partner then consider avoiding these activities for a while. Focusing your energy on the 20% of your partner's behavior that bothers you instead of the 80% of their behavior that honors you, is just a bad habit. And as such, it can be broken. Realistically you may have to avoid the people who encourage you to "vent" for a while. Maybe they haven't even been encouraging your venting but quietly tolerating it. So the new habit might come as a relief to them too. If it doesn't and your whole relationship was founded on mutual complaining (also known as "commiserating"), just find new friends. Life's too short to hang out with complainers.

# Habit 5 - Put On Your Own Oxygen Mask First

This might seem like strange advice on a book about maintaining love, respect, and vitality in your marriage, but here it is. For the long term success of your relationship, you need to get a little selfish.

You know when you're on a plane, and they are giving you emergency survival tips? Here's the first piece of advice you get. In the case of an emergency, put on your own oxygen mask first, before trying to help others. And so it is with your relationship. There will be many demands on your time and energy, but you will be unable to keep up with these demands and give the attention you need to nurture your relationship if you don't take care of yourself first.

Don't panic. This chapter is not going to turn into a diatribe of how you should be eating better, exercising and sleeping more (you should, but you already know that). Taking care of your needs goes deeper than getting a good night's sleep. Let's explore some areas of "self-care" that will have a direct impact on your relationship.

Keep Up Your Health

Obviously, if you are constantly sick and tired it will take a toll on your relationship. First, you won't be much fun to be around. Second, it will affect your libido. Third, it will affect your self-esteem which, in turn, will effect... well, everything. As a general rule, when you don't feel good about yourself, you don't feel good about anything.

This isn't a book about physical health and diet. I am assuming you know the basic principles of what it takes to have a healthier body. You need to eat well (avoid processed foods as much as possible), you need to keep your body moving (exercise) and you need to get a good night's sleep.

This all sounds simple, but I know it isn't easy. There will be plenty of times in a relationship when you will be in "survival mode". Kids will be sick, schedules will be hectic, parents grow old and needing care, money will be tight, and tempers will be frayed. The hormonal and physical changes alone that happen to our bodies over the course of a 20 year plus relationship are hard to deal with. There will be many "phases" that you go through on your journey together. There will be times when fast food is your only option, 3 hours of uninterrupted sleep seems like a luxury, and the suggestion that you are going to "nip out for a quick run" will not be met with a polite response.

I understand all of this. We all live in the real world. But the point that I want to make is that MANY people fall into the bad habit of putting everyone else's needs first. Not just in times of "survival mode", but as the norm. Women seem especially guilty of this. They consider it their duty and a virtue. And in the long run, it is a mistake. You must TAKE  RESPONSIBILITY for your own health. You are doing no one in your family any favors by being constantly depleted and frazzled. You will get sick and resentments will brew. And these are key ingredients in an unhealthy relationship.


Keep Up Your Interests

In her book Mating In Captivity, Ester Perel asked couples across 27 countries "When do you feel most turned on by your partner?" and "When do you feel most turned on yourself?"

The response was almost always the same: people feel attracted to their partner when they see them "in their element", doing something they accomplished and excited by. The feeling of watching someone from a distance and being proud of them that sparks attraction. Similarly, when people  are engaged in something at which they feel competent, they love doing, when they're "in the zone", they feel turned on by life and more turned on in general.

You can watch an excellent TED Talk on her research by checking the resources at the end of this book. It covers this information, as well as the ideas I discussed in Habit 3 about "responsibility and desire butting heads" and the need for both novelty versus familiarity in your love making. It is a 20-minute crash course in successfully maintaining desire in long term relationships, and I highly recommend it.

So, keeping up your interests is important for your self - image, and the image that your partner has of you. What else?

We all know people who, when they start a new relationship, suddenly morph into a new version of themselves that is strangely like their partner. Suddenly they take up all their partner's interests. While it's important to have shared interests, you should have interests that are uniquely your own. Not your partner's. And not your children's. Ladies, we can be especially guilty of this. I know so many women in their 40's or 50's who, once their children are older and more independent, have a little more free time to themselves but no idea what to do with it. Their lives, for 15 - 20 years had revolved around their children's interests, driving them to events or practice and being the best "snack mom" on the team. I remember asking someone once after a divorce, "Well, what do you like to do?" and she said, "I honestly can't remember. Maybe I should think about getting back into shape." Don't be that person.

Here's a final note on this: I know a charming couple who have been married for over 60 years. The gentleman in question is a very accomplished scientist who volunteered at my school for years after he retired. He was a man who always impressed me with his energy and varied talents and interests. I once asked him to what he attributed the success of his marriage. He said, "One thing is that I have lots of hobbies. My wife told me before I retired that I had better find some hobbies or I would be a very boring old man."

## Keep Up Your Friendships

No one person can meet all of your needs. It's lovely to believe in the idea of one perfect soul mate that can meet all of our emotional, intellectual, physical and sexual needs. But it's unlikely that we'll meet such a mythical creature. We live in the real world where amazing love and companionship isn't so much "found", but created between two people who fall in love and commit to continually work on their relationship.

Understanding this, it's easy to see that maintaining individual friendships when you are married is important. Men and women are different. We communicate differently, and our brains relax and decompress in different ways. It is not an oversimplification to say that women need to have girlfriends with whom they can talk about their feelings and create things with (scrap booking, quilting, baking, crafting). Likewise, men needs friends with whom they can just sit and have a beer with, go hunting, fishing, camping, golfing, shoot hoops with, or fix and build stuff with, no deep conversations about thoughts and feelings required.

As well as fulfilling different needs that men and women have, friendships become important safe and neutral places if your relationship does go through a rough patch. Sometimes you need to talk things through and get advice without wanting to confide in your family.

Keep Up Your Preferences - Advocate For Your Needs

Truly taking care of yourself involves more than just getting enough sleep and making time to keep up with your interests and your friends. One of the most important ways to ensure that you remain energized in your relationship is to advocate for your needs. It is important for you to have healthy habits around stating what you need you from your partner and your relationship. Good habits include finding the right way and time and have the conversation before resentments build up. If you don't express what you need at the appropriate time and the appropriate way, your small issue will become a ticking time bomb that will explode at an inappropriate time and, most likely, inappropriate way.

Let me give you an example of how you can advocate for your needs in an appropriate way.

1. Begin with a recognizing or appreciating something that your partner is delivering on or something in your relationship that is working well.

2. State what you need in a confrontational way. Usually with "I statements". That means instead of making someone defensive by saying "You do this and you do that", use statements that begin with "I".

"I feel more secure and respected when you show up on time or text me when you are going to be late."

3. Engage your partner in coming up with possible solutions to the issue. Don't just tell them what you want or expect, but ask them, "How do you think we can fix this?" Obviously  you probably already know the outcome you want, but engaging someone in coming up with the solution will be more effective in getting their "buy in".

Here's an example. It's starting to bother you that your partner is not letting you know when they are running late. They always have a good reason as to why they're late home (traffic, missed train, customer issue coming up at the last minute), but you are frustrated at the lack of communication.

Here's the inappropriate way to handle the situation. Let's say that this has happened a few times and has been bothering you for a while, but you haven't mentioned it. Maybe you just hoped it would go away. Maybe you are reluctant to "make waves" if you have a tendency to avoid conflict in general. In any event, the third time in a row it happens you yell at your partner when they come in the door.

"You always do this! You never call when you are going to be late! You have no respect for me! Dinner is cold ,and the kids keep asking me when you are going to be home!"

Here's a more appropriate way to handle this. The trick is, you need to handle it when before you get to the "I'm so mad I can't take it anymore" stage.

"Sweetheart, you know that I love when we get to sit down together and eat as a family. I appreciate being updated on exactly what time you think you'll be home so that I can make sure that dinner doesn't get cold or that we have to rush to eat as soon as you walk in the door. It's hard for me to plan when I don't know if you are running late. What do you think we can do about this?"

Whether it's getting your needs met in a practical way (needing more help with chores, or needing more sleep), an emotional way (needing more time alone with your partner) or even getting your needs met in the bedroom, following the three step formula above is definitely a more resourceful approach than just ignoring an issue and hoping it goes away.

Avoid The Deadly Mental Tally Sheet

There are two dangers with not advocating for your needs. The first, as I outlined above, is that by not addressing your needs in an appropriate way, you run the risk of expressing them in an inappropriate way. The second danger is that by not expressing your needs, little resentments build up and, you subconsciously start keeping a mental tally sheet. I wrote about the dangers of a mental tally sheet in <u>One New Habit To Fix Your Marriage</u>. Let me just quote directly from that book.

"One more note about math and numbers. Are you and your spouse champion score keepers? You know. Keeping a mental running tab, like your marriage is some sort of competition. Here are some of the areas that couples find themselves keeping score over:

- who slept less

- who works more hours

- who does more chores

- who takes on more of the responsibilities with   your children

- whose job/life is stressful in general

- who spends more "free time" hanging out with their friends or

- pursuing their hobbies

- who spends more of the disposal income (or who racks up more of  the debt)

- which spouse's family you spend more time with

Here's the danger with keeping score. It turns your marriage into some sort of competition. And in a competition, someone has to win. And in a marriage, if one person is winning, you are BOTH losing."

**One New Habit - Sacred Commitment To Honor Yourself**

1. Think of one area that you have been "suffering in silence" in your marriage. Commit to talking to your partner about this issue today using "non combat communication".

2. Schedule something just for yourself within the next two weeks - it can be anything that supports your physical health (bike ride with friends, new class at the gym), your emotional health (girls night or boys camping trip) or even that supports your creative passions (take up a new hobby or learn something new).

3. While you have the calendar out, encourage your partner to schedule some time for themselves, too. This is the essence of teamwork: working together to make sure BOTH partners' needs are being met. It will ensure that resentments don't quietly build up.

4. If you didn't do it after Habit 3, do it now. Watch Ester Perel's TED Talk. I guarantee there will be something in there that strikes a chord with you and it will be quicker and easier than reading her book (and it's free).

# Habit 6 - Update Your Contract Annually

Before you got married, you probably had a very clear vision of what you wanted your marriage to be. Many couples, especially if they do some kind of pre-marriage counseling through a church, develop a Marriage Mission Statement. Whether or not you have a formal document, at some point you and your partner should have had a frank discussion about the goals of your marriage, and how you would support each other. At the very least, you probably wrote your wedding vows.

To keep your marriage vibrant and healthy, it is important that you take the time to discuss these ideas and goals on a regular basis. It's important to schedule a time where you reflect on what is working well in your relationship, and what could be working better. The time to talk and reflect about these things is when you are calm and had time to get your thoughts together. If you randomly wait until you are frustrated by something your partner is doing, then more than likely you will just have an argument.

It is natural that long term relationships go through many phases. The goals and "rules of engagement" that you have for your relationship before children come into the equation are not the same goals you have when children are young, when children become teens or even when, eventually, children leave home and you retire. Your individual and combined needs change and evolve, and it's important to keep checking in with each other to see what they are, and how they can be best met.

In order to support the evolving need and goals of your long term relationship, I suggest all couples set up an annual "contract review". You can call it whatever you want. Take the Marriage Mission Statement off the wall and give it a dust, or if you don't have one, set up a new "Marriage Constitution".

The important thing is that you schedule a regular date on which you do this and that you commit to doing at least one a year. You could choose your anniversary date or a random date. But it should be scheduled and considered a "sacred commitment" that you and your partner both adhere to, no matter what.

Now, I understand that the way I have described this process doesn't make it sound much like fun. So far I've made it sound as appealing as a trip to the dentist, or your annual performance review with your boss. But hang in there, let me show you that there is a way to do this that can make it not only effective but relatively pain -free.

Here's one idea. My ex husband and I originally met on New Year's Eve. For many years it was our habit on New Year's Eve to present each other with a list of our "Top 10 Moments of the Past Year". It was really fun to see which items we had in common. But I was always fascinated that every year there were a couple of things on his list that I could barely remember, but that were really important to him, and vice versa. It was always a natural progression after sharing the list to discuss what about the last year had worked, and what we would like to see handled differently in the upcoming year. OK, perhaps it *was* a little like a performance review. Because I definitely remember asking him,

"What do you love me doing and want me to continue?"
" What do you not appreciate me doing and what me to stop?"
"What would you like me to start doing?"

Regardless, a good discussion always followed, and it gave us an open forum to talk about what we needed and wanted from each other in the upcoming year.

So that's one place to start. A "Top 10 of the Past Year" and then asking those questions.

Another great habit would be to start your discussion by checking in on your Love Languages.
If you are unfamiliar with the concept of Love Languages, this next section is going to TRANSFORM your relationship with your partner.

The term Love Languages was coined by Dr. Gary Chapman in his book, The Five Love Languages. His book has been on the New York Times Best Seller List more than 300 times, and for good reason. In his book, Dr. Chapman explains how what people consider a "meaningful expression of love" differs, depending on their Love Language. For example, one person may feel loved when their partner brings them a gift, while
65

another may feel more loved by hearing the words "I love you". The problems arise when one person's way of expressing love differs from their partner's way of feeling loved.

For example, let's say that you feel loved when your partner helps you out around the house. That means you identify with the Love Language "acts of service". Your partner, however, identifies with the Love Language "tokens of love". Your partner may very well sit around on the couch half of the day believing that they are loving you up something fierce because they bring you roses once a month. The problem is not that your partner doesn't love you, it's that you speak different Love Languages. In this scenario, even though you are not feeling loved and appreciated, your partner doesn't understand why ("How could you not know I love you? I buy you flowers every month!")

There are two really good pieces of news here. First, it's really easy to determine what your Love Language is. You can go to http://www.5lovelanguages.com/profile/ and take a five minute assessment. It's simple and it's free. Obviously, your partner should also take the assessment to determine their primary Love Language.

Here are the 5 Love Languages. Maybe you already know which one will be your primary language, maybe you will be surprised. Many people are surprised to learn that their partner's Love Language is not what they thought. Hey, it's natural to love people the way WE want to be loved. But important to take the time to learn how YOUR PARTNER wants to be loved.

- Words of Affirmation
- Acts of Service
- Receiving Gifts
- Quality Time
- Physical Touch

The second piece of good news is that there are no profile matches (or mismatches) that are "deal breakers". That means that even if you and your partner have different Love Languages, it's relatively easy to learn how to make your partner feel loved in a way that is meaningful to them.

Now because your relationship goes through different phases, it's possible that your Love Languages will vary over time. Most people have a primary Love Language, but other languages are important to varying degrees. For example, if you have young children in the house, your Love Language in the area of needing help with "acts of service" is probably going to be higher for a period of time. That's why a good way to start off your "Annual Marriage Review" (you might want to think of a sexier name for it!) may be to check in on your Love Languages.

Also, get into the habit of asking this question frequently, not just once a year. I heard Dr. Chapman mention it in an interview one time, and I think it's such a powerful question.

"On a scale of one to ten, how full is your love tank feeling right now?"

and

"What can I do to fill it?"

I think either of these two strategies would be a great way to start off your "annual review". It sets the tone for both of you to have a respectful and reflective forum to discuss any concerns, and to ensure that you feel supported and loved moving forward.

## One New Habit - Sacred Commitments To Your Union

1. Determine the Love Language of both you and your partner at http://www.5lovelanguages.com/profile/

2. Agree on a date to have a "contract renewal" conversation.

3.  Determine at least three things you would like to see in your "Marriage Constitution". Don't expect your partner to come up with all the ideas. To be effective, it needs to have input and "buy in " from both parties.

# Habit 7 - Don't Play With Fire

The six habits I have outlined so far should set a very solid foundation for a love that continues to grow through nurturing, passion and respect. The ideas and tools I have presented are practical and relevant to both secular and faith based marriages.

I have put a strong focus on positive habits that you should adopt for the vitality and health of your relationship. However, equally important are habits that you should avoid. There are immediate "deal breakers" in your relationship such as abuse, addiction, and adultery. That should be obvious. But other habits that don't immediately seem so damaging can also prove to be dangerous to your relationship. These bad habits can put chinks in the foundation of your relationship that, over time, can cause the whole thing to come toppling down.

I call them "Tiny sparks that can turn into fire."

You are probably familiar with the expression, "Don't play with fire or you're gonna get burned."
Playing with fire might seem fun and thrilling, in a risky sort of way. Likewise, there are many little "innocent" seeming temptations that will come your way over the course of a long term relationship. While they might seem fun and inviting, this particular habit encourages you to view all of these temptations as potential fires. I

69

advocate steering clear of them at all costs, for risk of getting burned.

Here are some examples of activities that can potentially lead to problems in your relationship. These activities may seem like harmless distractions, especially if your relationship is going through a "rough patch". But they all have the potential to damage your relationship, and so it's safer just to avoid them.

- Responding or making "friend requests" on Facebook to ex-boyfriends or ex-girlfriends or people with whom you have flirted or been attracted to in the past (they are called "old flames" for a reason).

- Flirting with people on Facebook, on-line chat rooms, or via text.

- Flirting with people while on a business trip or when out of town. Finding yourself alone in a hotel room or other secluded venue with a co-worker of the opposite sex is never a good idea.

- Fantasizing about your exes or people you are attracted to while making love to your partner. Even though an element of fantasizing can be a healthy part of your intimate relations, it's safer to fantasize about celebrities or imaginary "perfect lovers" that you don't actually know.

Basically, this habit is about using your common sense. Just avoid situations that might lead to temptation.

And it is important to be honest with yourself as to what "temptations" really look like. The stereotype of businessmen cheating on their wives while they are out of town is no longer the norm. More and more marriages have been damaged by "emotional affairs" that require no travel. We all have the technology and opportunity required to have "emotional affairs" readily available in our homes.

Here's the truth.

*Anytime you are relying on some one outside your marriage to meet either an emotional or physical need that should be being met inside your marriage; you are cheating on your spouse.*

So something as simple as commiserating with someone of the opposite sex about problems in your relationship can be as dangerous as playing with fire. You are risking an "emotional affair" that can be every bit as damaging as a physical one.

Personally, I would feel less betrayed if my partner had meaningless sex with someone when they were drunk (old stereotype of cheating) than if he had spent months secretly texting and talking to someone and getting emotionally attached to them. The technology to emotionally "cheat" is now in our pocket. It's easy to do and has become a growing problem for many couples.

Just be smart and avoid putting yourself in these situations.

Here's a practical guideline to follow. If you are unsure if you are crossing a line or not, ask yourself, "Would I be comfortable with my partner reading this e-mail or text?" If the answer is "no", then don't send it. Make a movie in your mind of the worst possible conclusion to these kind of betrayals (you losing your partner and your family and probably even your home in a divorce) and play it in your mind when you are tempted to play with fire. You will soon realize that it is just not worth the risk.

It really is that simple, if you don't want to get burned, don't play with fire.

If you do find yourself being tempted, then you need to be honest about which of your needs are not getting met within your relationship. And then you need to talk to your partner honestly about it. Flirting with danger is never going to be a productive way to improve your situation.

Other than the temptation to flirt and emotionally stray, there are two other areas which can have the potential to damage your relationship. These are also "sparks" that can turn into fire.

The first has to do with lying and keeping secrets.

Now I know "lying" is a harsh word. Some people see lying as a spectrum of activities. At the low end of the spectrum are "white lies", or lies we tell to protect people's feelings. Here are some sample untruths that many would consider "white lies":

"No honey, those pants don't make you look fat."

"I was just checking e-mail." (as you rapidly close the browser window to a porn website)

"I bought it on clearance." (as you hide the receipt, or wait until your partner isn't looking to smuggle purchases in from the car)

I'm not a fan of white lies. I believe that either you have a casual relationship with the truth, or you don't. The problem with telling white lies is that it becomes a habit. And then it can be a slippery slope from there on out. It's easy for the untruths to get bigger.

Any type of secret that you keep from your spouse is also a type of lie. Secrets and lies are very damaging and should have no place in a healthy relationship. I think this quote aptly illustrates the danger.

*"Secrets are like stars. They're hot, volatile concentrations of energy ... massive stars collapse in on themselves, growing so dense that they create an immense gravitational vortex from which even light can't escape. They become black holes."* - Martha Beck

The second potential danger area has to do with your peer group.

Consider this. Do you spend time with friends and couples who are committed to the growth of their relationship?

Tony Robbins famously said, *"Your lifestyle is a reflection of the expectation of your peers."*
73

Does your peer group consist of people who have negative opinions and experiences around long term relationships? If it does, then you need to be mindful of this, and make sure that their attitudes do not become contagious.

We all know that 50% of marriages end in divorce (the figure is even higher for second and third marriages.) However, this means that, for better or for worse, 50% of couples manage to commit to their marriage. Make sure that some of these people are in your peer group.

.

**One New Habit - Sacred Practices**

1. Use your common sense. Remember that if you play with fire, you risk getting burned. Live by the rule of thumb, "If I would be uncomfortable with my partner reading this or hearing this conversation, I shouldn't be doing it."

2. Don't tell "white lies" or keep secrets. Secrets and lies have no place in a healthy relationship.

3. Take an inventory of your peer group. Do you have a healthy mix of happy, stable couples in your group of friends to balance out the friends and family members who may be struggling with their relationships? If you want to have a healthy, growth oriented relationship, it will be easier if you have couples around you who have the same goals. They can provide support and positive role models at times when your relationship is going through change or stress.

# Conclusion

If you have read any of my other habit books you might be familiar with this quote,

*"Knowledge is the booby prize of self-development."*
Bill Harris

What this means is, knowledge in itself isn't going to change your life. You can keep reading books, listening to seminars and advice, but nothing about your circumstances will change just because you have more knowledge. You have to ACT on that knowledge. That's why this book up as a set of practical habits that you can easily implement. It takes just 21 days to make a new habit "stick". Pick one of the habits in this book and commit to working with it for three weeks. Once it has become an automatic habit, pick another one to work on.

Here's the truth, you already have relationship habits. The question is, are they habits that set up your relationship for long term success and growth, or not?

I will end this book with the same thought that I started with. And that is that your relationship is a living entity that needs nurturing every day. All long term relationships go through "phases". Some phases are great, some are tough, but the most damaging ones are the ones that you remain indifferent to. You simply cannot put "working on your relationship" on hold until a more convenient time comes along. You need to "water your garden" every day or it will wither away from neglect. Adopting the simple relationship habits outlined in this book can help.

Whether your relationship is just getting started or is already in "full swing", these seven habits will help form the foundation for understanding, support, respect and ongoing passion as your love grows and matures. Life happens and challenges come along. But if you have a solid foundation and good relationship habits, a marriage crisis needn't be one of them. Make your marriage a priority to ensure it stays healthy and vibrant, and will never need "fixing".

I wish you all the best in life and love.

# Habit Recap

1. **Sacred Rituals and Sacred Spaces**

   Make your relationship a priority that you nurture daily. Ensure that your bedroom is a haven of peace and love and centered on your relationship.

2. **Sacred Acts**

   Keep intimacy alive and mutually rewarding.

3. **Sacred Time**

   Keep dating each other.

4. **Sacred Words**

   Communicate in ways that are productive and supportive of each other.

5. **Sacred Commitment to Self**

   Put your oxygen mask on first. Take care of yourself so that you can be a better partner.

6. **Sacred Commitment to your Union**

   Honor your partner's Love Language. Create and update your Marriage Contract.

7. **Sacred Practices**

   Act and speak with integrity and don't "play with fire."

# Bonus Chapter

As a special "thank you" for reading this book, I am including a short chapter of my best-selling One New Habit relationship book, <u>Fix Your Marriage - 10 Simple Steps to Put the Joy & Intimacy Back in your</u> Marriage. I hope you enjoy it!

**Beginning of Bonus Chapter**

**What's On Your List?**

Did you get out of bed this morning with the express intention of getting frustrated by your kids? Of course not! Did you do it anyway? Probably. (Hey, I have teenagers in the house. Maybe my experience is different from yours, but I doubt it.)

It's probably the same with your spouse. Don't assume they got out of bed thinking they wanted to spend their day irritating, frustrating and disappointing you. Maybe they did anyway but assume the best intentions.

If you are reading this book, the reality is probably that your spouse is also not thoroughly thrilled with the state of your marriage. In which event anything YOU do to put some good energy back into it will be very well received and will be more likely to elicit some positive changes from your spouse.

Take out a piece of paper or open a text file and start listing everything you appreciate about your husband or wife. Start with the stuff that is probably huge, but that you have started to take for granted. Are they reliable? Do they get up and go to work every day? Do they come home every night? Do they work hard to make sure your children's needs are taken care off? Do they keep the house clean and food in the fridge and clean laundry in your drawer?

Maybe at first, it will be hard to think of things. Keep that piece of paper or list handy. Every day for 30 days find at least five things that your spouse did that day that you appreciated. Even if it was only take out the trash and be polite to your mom when they answered the phone. Start digging back to the beginning of your relationship. List all the kind, fun things they did for you.

HERE'S THE KEY CONCEPT AGAIN -  BY COMMITTING TO THIS EXERCISE YOU ARE FOCUSING ON BEHAVIOR YOU WANT, NOT ON WHAT YOU DON'T WANT. This will change the energy in your thoughts about your spouse and your marriage. If you change the thoughts, chances are you can change the feelings. And then your actions will change. If your actions change, so will your spouses.

Now the other important part of this exercise is to share some of these thoughts of appreciation with your spouse. Let me explain why.

I have spent a lot of time to reading and researching theories and studies on marriage, attraction, and relationships. Time and time again much of the research always ends up with the same findings: women have a need to feel appreciated and men have a need to feel respected and admired.

For example, in his book <u>The Truth About Cheating</u> M.Gary Neuman shocked many people with his findings about male infidelity. Conventional stereotypes portray women as "straying" to fulfill an emotional need and men straying to fulfill a physical one (sex). However, Neuman's research when interviewing men who cheated on their wives found that in 88% of the cases the new object of the man's affection was neither prettier, younger or in better shape than their wife. In the majority of cases men said they had strayed because they felt lonely in their marriage, were lacking attention from their wives and had a need to feel admired. This is why the stereotype of the man who cheats with his secretary persists with the subordinate presumably "looking up" to and admiring their boss. Not necessarily because she is younger and cuter and comes to work all made and dressed up, as opposed to walking around the house in her "comfy pants."

So at the end of the day, it becomes vitally important to communicate to your spouse that they are appreciated and admired. It doesn't take much to do this. See below.

**Things To Do Today**

1. Start your list of things that you appreciate and enjoy about your spouse. Commit to adding to the list every day for 30 days.

2. Choose one thing to share with your spouse today. Write them a quick note or send them an unexpected text with just a simple, honest sentiment. Examples could be "I admire the way you always work so hard for our family without ever complaining. Thank you" or "I really appreciate how hard you work to make sure the kids look clean and neat when they leave the house in the morning. Thank you." These are all things that should not be taken for granted.

End of Bonus Chapter

# Get Your Geek On

Here is more information about the resources quoted in this book.

If you are reading this book as an ebook on a web enabled device (Kindle, tablet, computer or smart phone) just click on the links.

If you are reading this as a physical book, all of these videos and resources can be found on the www.OneNewHabit.com website. Go to the "Book Resources" tab and find this book.

"Sex Needs A New Metaphor." To watch Al Vernacchio's TED Talk google his name plus TED TALK

"Men are Microwaves & Women Are Slow Cookers." To watch Ted Cunningham's talk google his name plus TALK

Mating in Captivity: Unlocking Erotic Intelligence Esther Perel, 2007

To watch Ester Perel's TED Talk google her name plus TED TALK

Men Are from Mars, Women Are from Venus    Dr. John Gray, 1992

To watch Dr. Gray's TED Talk - "Mars Brain Venus Brain" just type the title plus Dr. Gray's name into your favorite browser

The Five Love Languages        Gary D. Chapman, 2009

To take a free assessment to determine your primary Love Language visit:
http://www.5lovelanguages.com/profile/

Living Like Newly Weds

26 Amazing Activities to Maintain
Connection in
Long Term Relationships

And one more time with feeling.... to download the free ebook that came with this book click on this image, or visit :
 http://www.OneNewHabit.com/marriage-gift/

# Good Karma

THANK YOU for buying this book. Book reviews are very important to me and to Amazon. They help us make books and your buying and reading experience better. If you liked this book, I would REALLY appreciate it if you take a few moments to review this book on Amazon.

**Things to do NOW :)**

Leave a review for this book on Amazon. com

LIKE my Facebook page and help create a community of fans commenting on how they are using these strategies. You'll get a little dose of happy in your FaceBook feed when you most need it. You can find it at : https://www.facebook.com/ OneNewHabit

# Also Available

Check out other books in the <u>One New Habit</u> Series:

What people are saying about this book:

*"I wish there was more (that's a compliment!) After getting mired down in a few books that spend chapters and chapters talking about brain-wiring, my damaged childhood (which wasn't), and the difference between the sexes... this book was very refreshing. Simple yet smart advice. Some "homework" and lists, but not complicated exercises. I found myself nodding. She gets it. And it's so concise and such an easy read, you would be doing yourself and your marriage NOT to read it."* Amazon 5 \*\*\*\*\* review

"She hit all the right notes. So many people focus on the negative and instead the author asks us to focus on the positive. The two minute movie in the the enhanced e-book was worth it in and of itself."

85

**The Happy Habit**

**10 SIMPLE HABITS**

Step By Step Guide To Finding More
Happiness & Joy In Your Life

Grace Stevens - One New Habit Series

What people are saying about this book:

*"While this is an "easy" read - the "simple" steps that the author outlines, and the questions she asks are truly thought-provoking. This is a quick and easy read that is loaded with facts, studies, and SIMPLE ways to get thinking about, and ACTING on your own path to happiness. The author's style is casual and informal - and very easy to read."*
Amazon 5 star ***** review

*"What can I say? I LOVED this little book. The question you need to ask yourself is are you happy right now? If not, do you want to be happy? If you answered "YES" to that second question this is the book for you."*

Amazon 5 star ***** review

What people are saying about this book:

*"This book provides easy steps to meditation in a concise manner. I liked the practical tips for incorporating it in your daily routine. I recommend it to anyone who would like to try meditation and needs a guide."*

*Amazon 5 \*\*\*\*\* review*

*"Grace has captured the essence of how you can get the most out of mindfulness.*
*She provides good scientific support of what a mindfulness practice can do for you.*
*She presents a welcome pragmatic guide that doesn't try to convince you of any way of thought.*

*Rather, she lovingly provides a tool kit full of implements for daily crafting of your own practice. …. Pragmatic and genuine."*

*Amazon 5 \*\*\*\* review*

STOP
PROCRASTINATING

9 SIMPLE HABITS

Step By Step - How To Regain
Control of Your Time and Your Life
In One FUN Filled Week

Grace Stevens · One New Habit Series

What people are saying about this book:

*"Another great book from Grace Stevens! Love the ideas broken down into small to-do items. Makes the information easy to understand and accomplish....which is key for an Anti-Procrastination book. Grace includes interesting examples and links to Ted talks (which I love!). She includes several different ways of understanding her information, which is great for every type of learner. LOVE her books....can't wait for more!"*

Amazon 5 star ***** review

*"To my surprise I found not one but many habits I can do right away. As I read the book, I put it down to set my timer and do a 20 minute power cleaning, I was feeling motivated ;). I specially like all the resources provided at the end of the book!"*
Amazon 5 star ***** review

# About The Author

*"What if you don't have the wrong intentions, you just have the wrong directions?"*

A self confessed "personal development geek," Grace Steven's books combine a mixture of current research and practical examples and tips, all in an easy to digest conversational tone. Lovingly, she provides the you right directions to have better relationships, more joy and inner peace.

In her One New Habit book series Grace breaks down seemingly overwhelming problems into simple, actionable steps - habits - that anyone can develop over time.

Grace lived and studied in four countries before making California her home. When not writing, she can be found on a yoga mat or a bike, outside having fun with her two teenagers and friends, or inside teaching her third graders to love learning and the importance of washing their hands. All of which serve to keep her from taking life, and herself, too seriously.

10060694R00051

Printed in Great Britain
by Amazon